DESERT WAR

A UNIQUE PHOTOGRAPHIC RECORD
OF THE DESERT RATS AT WAR

Photographs by Mike Moore

Foreword by Richard Kay

PENGUIN BOOKS

TO HARRY

PENGUIN BOOKS

Published by the Penguin Group
Penguin Books Ltd, 27 Wrights Lane, London W8 5TZ
Penguin Books USA Inc., 375 Hudson Street, New York, New York 10014, USA
Penguin Books Australia Ltd, Ringwood, Victoria, Australia
Penguin Books Canada Ltd, 2801 John Street, Markham, Ontario, Canada L3R 1B4
Penguin Books (NZ) Ltd, 182–190 Wairau Road, Auckland 10, New Zealand

Penguin Books Ltd, Registered Offices: Harmondsworth, Middlesex, England

This collection of photographs first published in book form 1991
10 9 8 7 6 5 4 3 2 1

Photographs copyright © Mike Moore, 1991
Foreword copyright © Richard Kay, 1991
All rights reserved

Origination by Anglia Graphics Ltd, Bedford
Printed in England by St Ives plc

Except in the United States of America, this book is sold subject
to the condition that it shall not, by way of trade or otherwise, be lent,
re-sold, hired out, or otherwise circulated without the publisher's
prior consent in any form of binding or cover other than that in
which it is published and without a similar condition including this
condition being imposed on the subsequent purchaser

CONTENTS

ACKNOWLEDGEMENTS

All my thanks to Colonel Iain Johnstone and the men of the First Royal Scots, especially Major John Potter, to whom I owe a great debt; to my picture editor, Ron Morgans, for assigning me to the Gulf in the first place; to Ken Lennox and Colin Davey for unselfishly transmitting my pictures to London; and to my wife Helen and my son Harry, who put up with so much.

And special thanks to Richard Kay of the *Daily Mail*, who was at my side the entire time, encouraging, helping, carrying, digging, washing, laughing and crying.

Mike Moore
22 March 1991

FOREWORD by Richard Kay

It was a terrible day to go to war. Rain had churned the sand into a gritty, pudding-like mud, while rockets streaked overhead across the sky. In the darkness red and white tracer hissed about our ears like a swarm of angry hornets, and all around us the explosion of shells sent great fountains of desert up into the air.

When the doors of our troop carrier had been thrown open, admitting the cold, the damp and, let's face it, the fear, there had been time only to exchange the briefest of gestures, a nod and a smile of encouragement. For us, both non-combatants at the very extremity of Britain's front-line action to liberate Kuwait, the hours that unfolded were a blend of exhilaration, privilege and, above all, relief.

After the Second World War it had been widely assumed that the next great conflict would be a push-button affair, in which individuals mattered little. When it began, the battle to drive Iraq back to its own frontiers was just that: Cruise missiles fired from an ocean hundreds of miles away and 'smart' bombs delivered with pin-point precision. Any suggestion that British troops might later peer across a no man's land of barbed wire, trenches and mines seemed absurd, an inconceivable return to the battlefields of 1916. Yet that was the undertaking that confronted the Desert Rats when they rolled into Iraq on the afternoon of 25 February 1991. That they achieved their task in half the allotted time is a tribute to their skills, courage and preparation.

As photographer and correspondent at the front, Mike Moore and I had been permitted to join a very exclusive club. Our assignment was not just the hundred-hour war and the euphoria that followed its end but also the weeks of preparation, training and waiting that led up to it. The Army has long been ambivalent about the presence of correspondents during its operations, but the role of the cameraman is regarded as paramount. The photographer first went to war in the Crimea, laden with bulky wooden

cameras and tripods, boxes of glass plates and bottles of chemicals. Mercifully, the equipment is lighter these days, but the role of the stills photographer remains central to the recording of conflict.

Our involvement had begun as the first missiles landed on Baghdad, when, dressed from head to toe in Army uniform, we joined the men of the 4th Armoured Brigade. Overnight we had to adjust to a soldier's routine of orders obeyed. For us this manifested itself mostly in trench digging. We developed an agreeable and effective system: while one of us swung the pickaxe into the ground, the other would spoon away the loose sand. We were proud of our trenches – the deeper the better – and the rhythmic thwack of pick on unyielding ground, the sound of Kay and Moore at work, became familiar to the soldiers.

As the days trickled by we were grateful for our early familiarization with desert craft. Our blisters were testimony not just to trench digging but also to putting up camouflage nets and balancing equipment on shoulders used to nothing heavier than a flannel suit.

Daylight hours were precious for our official work – there was no artificial light – so we were happy to do our Army duties after nightfall. That willingness had an unexpected side effect that was as positive and beneficial as anything that we recorded on film and in notebook. In the early days of the crisis soldiers were used to journalists appearing for a day in the desert before retreating to the hot water and comfort of Saudi Arabian hotels. We lived as the soldiers did, sleeping in shell-scrapes with them and eating the same reheated Army food. We were also volunteers, who wanted to be there with them – and that seemed to count. The camaraderie extended to us by the soldiers, particularly the infantry of The Royal Scots, was a source of both inspiration and immense pride.

Of course, trust and tolerance develop naturally when,

for forty-eight hours at a time, men are compressed into the back of an armoured Warrior personnel carrier, where there is no room for any exaggerated movement – such as standing up. On the eve of war Mike and I discovered this when we learned that another soldier was to share our cramped living space in the Warrior. In vain we had made every possible effort to pare down our possessions to the miserable level of the soldiers' belongings. We could cope with the intense heat generated by uniform, chemical suit, flak jacket and no ventilation. We could cope with the bottom-numbing discomfort. We could even cope – just – with the realization that the Desert Rats were tasked to fight at night, which was hardly conducive to the finest photography. What we could not handle at first was the very idea of squeezing another human being into that claustrophobic sardine can...

We managed, however, and for us, as for past generations of men at the front, wartime forged great friendships. When you have watched someone having an all-over body wash with a thimbleful of cold water – and been watched yourself – you have few secrets. We shared everything with our new friends: food parcels, water, field gear, letters from home, even superstitions. We shared the cooking after we moved from the luxury of cookhouse food to preparing it ourselves in grenade tins over a gas stove until the gas ran out. A last-minute trade with the Americans had provided us with enough boil-in-the-bag rations for four days of fighting. We shared moments of high drama – like the occasion when we were trapped for hours in a suspected mine field only to be informed by an irate sapper that the 'mines' were the burrows of real desert rats – and hours of stupefying boredom.

When the men were told to prepare themselves for the awfulness of battle we listened too. We attended their briefings, at which the tension rose perceptibly by the day. We were affected by their sadness about the pitifully inadequate army that had been sent to oppose us. One section of this book deals with the real price of modern warfare: the destruction and the dead.

But there were moments of humour: it was difficult to take too seriously the plight of the colonel who, just before news of the cease-fire reached us, had ordered his men to knock all the glass out of the Landrovers and trucks as a battle precaution. 'Now where am I going to find two hundred windscreens?' he wailed.

This, then, is the record of Britain's winter war in the desert, fought in harsh rain, choking dust and temperatures that dropped below freezing at night. From his unique perspective as the only cameraman with the front-line forces, Mike Moore has assembled a remarkable portrait of a modern army at work. War photography has always produced pictures of melancholy beauty: Moore's achievement is that he has also managed to capture the warmth of comradeship, the discipline of a highly trained force and the humanity that survives brutal conditions. No accompanying narrative is necessary: the photographs speak for themselves.

WAITING

Vincent, seventeen: too young
to vote, too young to serve in
Northern Ireland...

DAILY LIFE

Early on, the living is easy and the
food good

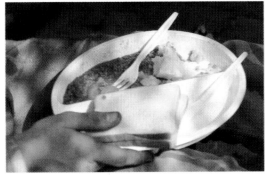

The all-over body wash and
the only proper shower in two
months

Washday luxury at the rear
echelon – but even during private
moments a soldier's gas mask is
on his hip

Yet another jab: this time against
plague

Headshaving

The rigours of foot inspection

TRAINING

Cas-evac practice at Dressing
Station 5 Alpha

'Pulling through': barrel-cleaning
on an M109 field gun

THE LEADERS

Lieutenant-General Sir Peter de la Billière

Defence Minister Tom King

Brigadier Christopher Hammerbeck

Brigadiers Ian Durie and
Christopher Hammerbeck: the
shepherd's crook and the leather
gloves are their hallmarks

Plans: the Brigade HQ

Brigadiers Patrick Cordingley and
Christopher Hammerbeck and
Major-General Rupert Smith attend
a briefing

FORMING UP

The final briefings begin for The
Royal Scots: a pensive Major John
Potter, B Company Commander,
receives his orders

Major Norman Soutar, A Company
Commander, The Royal Scots

Lieutenant-Colonel Iain Johnstone,
Commanding Officer, 1st Battalion
The Royal Scots, gives his last
night briefing

The men of The Royal Scots
receive their orders

EVE OF BATTLE

The padre, Stephen Blakey, leads his congregation

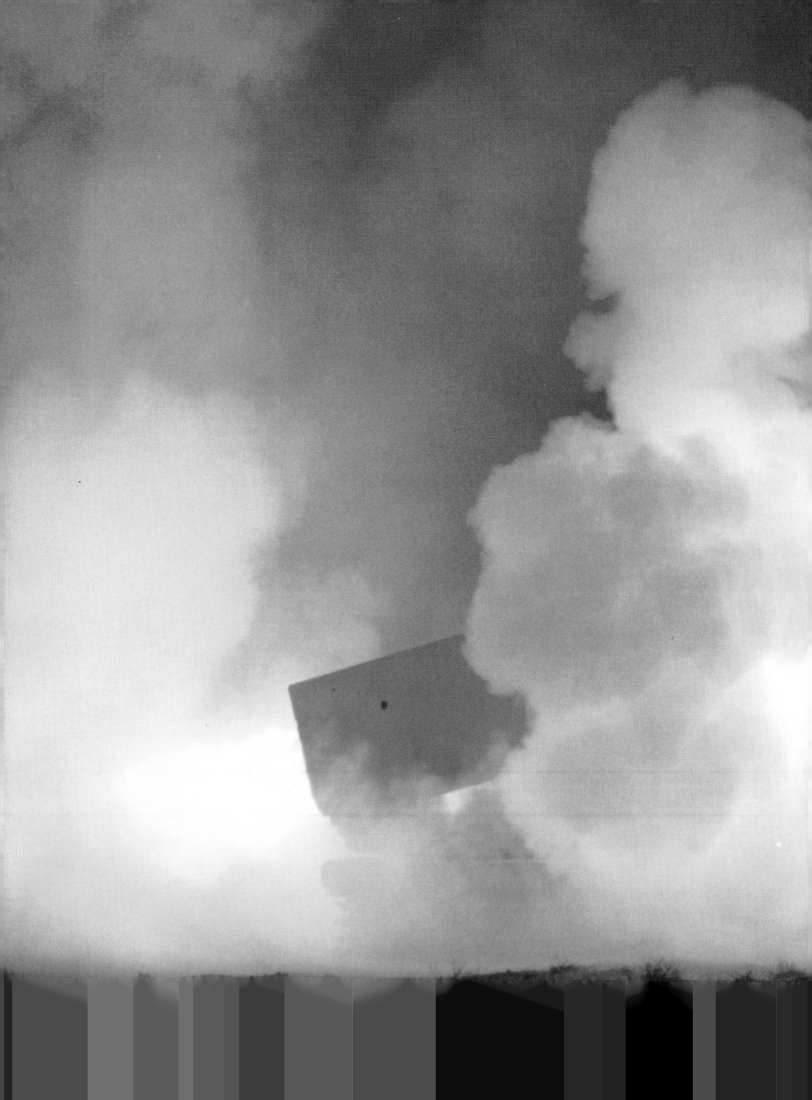

ACTION

The opening salvos from the Multi-Launch Rocket System of the Royal Artillery

Sergeant Tom Gorrian leads 5 Platoon, B Company, The Royal Scots, against an Iraqi armoured personnel carrier buried to its turret in the sand

With a grenade, Sergeant Gorrian
advances on the enemy position

Taken out

Major John Potter with the
prisoners

THE PRICE

Men of the Burial Detail clear the battlefield

The bodies of Iraqi soldiers
awaiting burial

The road to Basra

Kuwait – a liberated city shrouded
in smoke from burning oil fires

The remains of British Airways
Flight 149, trapped at Kuwait
Airport on 2 August 1990

THE END

Unused beds at the 33rd Field
Hospital

Celebration

Challenger tanks leaving the front